*Journey Through Heartache*

# *Journey Through Heartache*

Charlene Roberson Chandler

Copyright © 2006 by Charlene Roberson Chandler.

Cover design by Anna Leah Hormiguera.

Library of Congress Control Number:    2006903844
ISBN:          Softcover              1-4257-1412-9

All rights reserved. No part of this book may be reproduced or transmitted in any form or by any means, electronic or mechanical, including photocopying, recording, or by any information storage and retrieval system, without permission in writing from the copyright owner.

This book was printed in the United States of America.

To order additional copies of this book, contact:

870-768-3479
crobchandler@sbcglogal.net

# Contents

Acknowledgments ................................................................. 9

Forward ................................................................................ 11

1. How Do We Find Happiness .............................................. 13

2. Have You Tried Prayer ..................................................... 27

3. Don't Cry For Me ............................................................... 41

4. The Search For Tomorrow ................................................ 57

5. Balance The Scale ............................................................. 65

About the Author ................................................................. 71

Endnotes .............................................................................. 73

To My Son
Mark

# Acknowledgments

Permission is gratefully acknowledged from the following:

References from May, 1973 Guideposts article Get Rid of Resentment by Dr. James A. Stringham, Houston, Texas. Reprinted with permission from Guideposts. Copyright 1973 by Guideposts, Carmel, New York 10512. All rights reserved.

Mrs. Wanda McIntosh's name. Used by permission.

References from the Power of Positive Praying by John Bisagno. Copyright 1965 by Zondervan Publishing House. Used by permission.

References from works of Dr. Norman Vincent Peale and Ruth Stafford Peal: Thought Conditioners, Love Comes First in Creative Living, Insight That Sees Through Confusion, and This Thing Called Guidance. Copyright Peale Center. Used by Permission.

# Forward

On April 28, 1984, I married a truly wonderful man in the beautiful little chapel of First United Methodist Church in Marianna, Arkansas.

My twenty-eight-year-old, six-foot-one, son flew home from Alaska to be "father of the bride." We took him back to the airport prior to leaving on a short honeymoon. As my son and I were walking down the long wide corridor of the airport terminal, I took that opportunity to spend a few minutes alone with him before he left while my new husband checked on flight schedules. One of his concerns as he grew up had been that I was alone and not getting any younger, so in trying to reassure him, I said, "You finally got your mother raised; I'm all grown up now and you have me safely married so you don't have to worry about me anymore." I think the next few moments are moments that we, as parents, treasure forever. He looked over at me with those big brown eyes and in an expression more serious than amused said, "Yeah, and it's been a long hard trip!"

As his boyhood years flashed before me, I realized that as difficult as it had been to raise a child alone, it probably had been harder on him than me. For him, growing up had been a long hard trip. And that's what my search for happiness has been: It's been a long hard trip! As you read through the heartache and tears, the journey, adventure and joys, you will sometimes laugh; those who know and love me may sometimes cry. But through it all, as you see in my life the inestimable value of what I have learned from others, one great universal truth will stand out: That however exciting the adventures of life may be along the way, our search for happiness may be a long and tedious path that sometimes carries us to a—Journey Through Heartache.

# Chapter 1

## HOW DO WE FIND HAPPINESS

When our life is in a shambles, we may ask, **"How did I get to the place where I am?** Lord, this is not where I want or intended to be." But if we look back into the intricate tapestry of our life, we can see it was one small step at a time with each heartbreaking choice in the wrong direction that has brought us to the place where we are.

It is so easy to blame others for our circumstances or conditions in life, which at times may seem like a struggle just to survive. And most of the time we say, "It is your fault. You or they did this or are doing this to me!" Therefore, at what point do we stop blaming others for our unhappiness or failures.

I reached this point at about age thirty-seven when I began to learn that the quality of life or true happiness does not have to be diminished by the injustices inflicted upon us by others. It depends upon the condition of our inner being, our relationship to God, and how we react to each situation or circumstance. Over the years, I learned this:

(1) We act or react to any given situation according to the kind of person we are.
(2) The kind of person we are is determined by the condition of our inner being.
(3) And the condition of our inner being is governed by the quality of our relationship to God, or the lack of it.

Some may not even care about the quality of their inner being or whether they have a relationship with God so long as their own selfish desires are fulfilled, thus they become the cause of many problems and grief for others instead of being part of the world's cures.

Life's problems are myriad. Many may be trapped in unhappy marriages or other heartbreaking situations: Poverty, hard grinding jobs, or the inability to change a difficult situation. Some suffer financial distress through no fault of their own or because of poor management, poor choices, lack of motivation, or just plain laziness. The list is endless. But many of these situations, heartbreaking as they are, pale in comparison to the heartache of parents who have had children stolen, children with terminal diseases, handicapped children, or children who have ruined their lives with dope and involvement in crime. Again, the list is endless.

Therefore, choices, even little ones, are so important! When we make bad choices, we literally become the victim of our own poor judgment and eventually end up in a situation or circumstance not to our liking. Even what appears to be seemingly small insignificant choices at the time can have lasting, immeasurable, and devastating effects. It's like passing by our exit on the interstate. To find an exit, we may have to go many miles before we can get off. So it is as we travel through the journey of life. If we make a wrong choice, it may takes years of hard work, trials, or heartache before there is an exit; and sometimes there are no exits and the consequences of our choices create circumstances that lasts a lifetime. A good example is an unwanted pregnancy or those condemned to imprisonment for life for their crimes.

Unfortunately some of us did not learn, when we were very young, how important choices are and made many wrong ones. It is our own choices most of the time that control the circumstances of not only our daily life but our ultimate eternal destiny. When we stand before God to be judged, it will not matter what others did that adversely affected our life. God holds us accountable only for what we do, and we will be judged accordingly. Therefore, we are responsible for how we act or react in any given situation or towards any person.

So much unhappiness and bitterness is created within the family structure and society because of petty arguments, grievances, et cetera. Yet, we become involved in these in the course of daily life with emotions and inferiorities governing behavior patterns. We are quick to criticize and find fault with others, but it is difficult to see our own. Why? Perhaps the quality of our relationship to God is not what it should be.

How do we know our relationship to God is what it should be? Simply put, this quality is measured by how we treat others, whether it is family, friends, enemies, or humanity as a whole. Do we hate, bear grudges, hold resentments and unforgiveness in our heart? It is difficult to comprehend that how we act or behave in adverse situations is not caused by what someone else does. Yes, we can always say if he, she, or they had not said or done that, I wouldn't have done what I did. But this is the whole point! We don't have to let what others say or do control our behavior. When we react on an emotional level to what others do, we become as puppets to the puppeteer. They pull the string (say or do something), and we react accordingly. Literally, in these cases, we let others control our lives. Do we really want others to control what we do?

We do not have to act or react according to circumstances or situations. We can choose how we act, react, or behave. How? First, decide how we want to act and what kind of person we truly want to be; but most important consider what kind of person God wants us to be and work toward that goal. Can we do it on our own? Probably not. Most of the time we can't, but we can through the great power of God, through the Holy Spirit. I believe that we can rid our self of any unwanted habit, no matter how bad it is if we truly want to and call upon the Holy Spirit to help us. This help may be strength through the Holy Spirit or guidance to special programs. These habits could include excessive drinking, addictions, over-eating, bad temper, foul speech, gossiping, and harboring grudges and resentment, et cetera.

It has been said that speech is the mirror of the soul. Do we like the condition of our inner being as reflected by our speech or actions? In the human drama of life, each of us is the star, the leading lady or man who has the starring role. If we stand back and view our self as if we were watching a movie, what would we see in our actions, behavior, and character portrayal? Would we be pleased?

When my son Mark was about fourteen, we were putting carpet down one day. Sadly, many parents yell at their children. I was yelling do this, do that, when all of a sudden my up-to-this-point extremely patient son yelled at me. I said in a hurt voice, "Honey, that is no way to talk to your mother." His reply, "That's the way you talk to me," brought me up short. Here was this child that I loved more than life itself, and I spoke many times unkindly to him.

I realized then that the quality of my inner being was not what it should be. I decided right then and there that I would never raise my voice to my child again. It took three years of practicing to always speak, no matter how irritated I was, in a kind soft tone of voice. But breaking a bad habit is worth the effort and the rewards are many. After several months, I no longer had the desire to yell at my son, even as irritating as teenagers can be. But the greatest reward of all is that I have seen these qualities of patience and kindness emerging in him as he grew into adulthood.

It takes a concerted effort to control our own behavior or speech. It is necessary to practice that dirty word self-discipline. We cannot change others; we can only change our self. When I concentrate on correcting my own deficiencies, I do not have time to concern myself with the faults of others. Others may do or say things that bring tears to our eyes or deep hurts into our life. We may not be able to change or control this pain, but we can control how we respond, how we behave. How? Practicing love is the key.

"Whatever you do in life, do with love!" says the late Dr. Smiley Blanton, noted psychiatrist and co-founder of the American Foundation of Religion and Psychiatry in New York City in his unforgettable book **Love or Perish,**[1] which is, unfortunately, now out of print. I learned many things from Dr. Blanton's book, but most important was the priceless lesson that so often we spend our time trying to grasp love when we should instead concentrate on the giving of love. We cannot make others love us; it is in the giving of genuine love that we receive love in exchange. Dr. Blanton said that as important as it is to have love, it is even more important to give love. "For we must love—or Perish."

This book, its pages now yellowed with time, is one of my most treasured book. I look back in amazement at how it came into my possession. It was in 1967 when I was recuperating from major surgery that my sister Mozelle suggested I read Norman Vincent Peale's book **The Power of Positive Thinking.**[2] I was most impressed and began reading all of Dr. Peale's books. I came to love Dr. Peale through his works and even started receiving his monthly printed sermons. I received them for more than thirty years.

In his works, Dr. Peale referred to Dr. Blanton as one of the great teachers and lovers of humanity. I was fascinated by Dr. Blanton as portrayed by Dr. Peale and thought what a truly wonderful experience it would be to know or just meet such a man. I was saddened by the fact that this would never be possible as Dr. Blanton had already passed away. Later in one of Dr. Peale's printed sermons called **Love Comes First in Creative Living**[3] he referred to Dr. Blanton's book **Love or Perish,** a book that I did not even know existed. I was so excited that I went to the bookstore and immediately ordered one. Even though I will never meet Dr. Blanton himself, I feel that I was able to know him in a very special way through his book.

Later, more copies were ordered and given to friends. Even later more copies were ordered, and this book was then out of print. I marvel at the timing of events that take place. Had I not found out about this book when I did, it would not have been available to me. The impact upon my life in subsequent years, because of the insights revealed therein, have been incalculable.

Since that time, through years and studies of the works of many, I have learned more about what love really is, not only relating to human relationships but to God's love which we call Christian love. What is Christian love? Christian love is an unselfish love that ultimately governs the quality of our individual relationships involving all others. When we care enough about pleasing God to express love with no expectation of receiving anything in return, that is Christian love. It is putting the needs and welfare of others before our own. This is the love that enables us to **act instead of reacting**, even to those who have done us an injustice. Realistically, how can we put this into practice? It isn't easy, but it can be done.

God's commandment is to love. This does not mean to express love only when surrounded by congeniality and the lovely but to express love to others in all circumstances, including the poor, the neglected, the unlovely. How? By practicing the following:

> *(4) Love is very patient and kind, never jealous or envious, never boastful or proud, (5) never haughty or selfish or rude. Love does not demand its own way. It is not irritable or touchy. It does not hold grudges and will hardly even notice when others do wrong. (6) It is never glad about injustice, but rejoices whenever truth wins out. (7) If you love someone you will be loyal to him no matter what the cost. You will always believe in him, always expect the best of him, and always stand your ground in defending him (1 Corinthians 13:4-7 LB).*

If our expressions of love do not reflect the above characteristics, we have little or no real love for others. **But loving a person should not be confused with liking them.** It is impossible to like some people because of the kind of person they are. To love a person means to sincerely want the best for them in spite of not liking them. Where then do we get this love? Ask God for it. This may never change how the other person feels about us, but it can change our feelings toward them. Over a period of time, we may reach a point where we do not dislike them and our expression of love will be more genuine.

When our relationship to others is examined in the light of Christian love, we may realize just how little love we have or give. Some give only in proportion to what is received, or less. It is possible to do good things for others without loving them, so we should make sure we do not fall into the trap of thinking that we are doing something out of love when in reality we are doing it in the hope that we will receive something in return or some future reward from God.

It takes an honest soul-searching evaluation of our own motives to distinguish the difference. We should purify our motives by looking within as the first step toward expressing love because we actually love that person or want to please God rather than expressing love in the hope of receiving some personal benefit from it. This benefit may be only the praise of others. But all gifts without love equals nothing of enduring value. The gift itself is temporary; but love that motivates the giving of a gift or love expressed during a relationship, even though that relationship no longer exists, is what endures. This is what helped me to understand what the old adage has said over and over: Only love last forever!

It has been said that you cannot measure love, but this is not true. This is easily determined. Our love for others is measured by how we treat them; our love for God is also measured by how we treat our fellowman. This includes family and friends, as well as all others. I used to tell God just how much I loved him; and every time I did this, he said, "Do you love old so and so?" And, you know, he picked out the one person in the whole world that I just couldn't stand. Sadly, I had to say, "No, Lord, I don't love that person." And God said, "Then you don't love me."

And last, how do we keep on loving those who do us injustices day in and day out and cope with the pettiness of others in daily life? There is only one way that I know. Remember that they too are loved by God and **Learn the Value of Forgiving!**

On a beautiful sunny day in 1989, the courtroom was packed as proceedings were about to begin. This was criminal pre-trial day when criminal cases would be set for the fall term. As an official court reporter for the First Judicial Circuit of Eastern Arkansas, I sat at my desk ready and waiting for court to begin when Wanda,[4] the Circuit Clerk, walked over to my desk and, in a voice filled with anger and bitterness, said, "Look at him! Look at him! He's sitting there in the front row smirking because he knows he isn't going to jail; he's laughing at me because he's getting away with it. The prosecutor has agreed to reduce his charge, and he will only get a five-year suspended sentence!"

This scene had been repeated during the past year and a half as Wanda poured out the story of how this young man had embezzled $100,000 from her father, ruining his business and forcing him into bankruptcy, how this had affected her parents, the harm done to her family as a whole as a result of this financial distress, and to herself.

A sense of helpless frustration engulfed me as I sat thinking: What can I do to help Wanda? What possible solution can there be for such an injustice or all the injustices of the world, for that matter? Obviously, the young man was not going to be punished; and even if he were, this would not restore the money nor the business. Obviously, too, listening and sympathizing, however comforting, was not a solution to the problem. Suddenly, appalled at my own abruptness, unbidden and unasked for, five words came out of my mouth. I said quietly, "Wanda, you have to forgive." Her reply was, "I can't forgive. Look what he has done. He has hurt my parents, my family, me, and even the church because now my parents can't contribute as much to the church."

All that day during every recess and the lunch hour, Wanda and I talked about forgiveness, what it means, how it affects us, and how we can forgive even in a situation like this. And standing there at my desk that same day, because she is a fine Christian lady sincerely wanting to live for God, Wanda said, "Lord, I forgive." Has forgiving made a difference in Wanda's life? A year later, I asked her, and she honestly said, "I still feel the man should be punished, and there is still a little bitterness in my heart, but not the deep anger and bitterness that I once had."

Listed below are the five steps of forgiving that I shared with Wanda that day that I had so tediously learned from the works of others over the many years and applied to my own life:

1. **What is Forgiveness?** Forgiveness, in its simplest form, means not to hold something someone has done against them.

    It is difficult to ask God for forgiveness for our own wrongdoing. It is even more difficult to forgive others. In the first place, we do not want to forgive them; and we hold onto and enjoy to some extent that hurt, pain, or humiliation we suffered. We say, "Look what they did, the injustice they did us, how they hurt us. I can't forgive." But how bad was it? Sometimes it's very bad and the consequences are tragic and devastating; but when we think about how God forgives us no matter what we do, how can we not forgive others?

2. **Why is it so important to forgive?** The very most important reason is that God will not forgive us unless we also forgive others:

> *(14) For if ye forgive men their trespasses, your heavenly Father will also forgive you. (15) But if ye forgive not men their trespasses, neither will your Father forgive your trespasses (Matthew 6:14-15 KJV.)*

When we have asked God to forgive us, we assume all is well and we are forgiven; but so long as we hold unforgiveness toward others in our heart, our own sins are unforgiven. That's a difficult thing to understand and maybe accept, but this Scripture emphatically states we have to forgive if we want to be forgiven. Another important reason to forgive is that when we do not forgive others, we hold resentment, anger, grudges, hate, and bitterness in our heart. This "adversely affects us," sometimes even our physical health. All these things hurt us, not the person toward which they are directed because they probably don't care how we feel about them. Our attitudes in life in general are also adversely affected, and so is our relationship to God. Relationships between husbands and wives, mothers and fathers, brothers and sisters, other family members, and friends can be marred or totally destroyed.

None of us can rid our self of resentment unless we know what resentment is. What is resentment? Dr. James A. Stringham, a renowned psychiatrist of Houston, Texas wrote an article in the May, 1973 Guidepost entitled **Get Rid of resentment**[5] in which he says that the word resentment is derived from two Latin words which mean "to feel again." He said that when we resent something, we feel the same hurt or anger that we felt when an event occurred even though it may have happened years in the past.

Dr. Stringham goes on to say that it doesn't matter how justified the resentment is; that the effect on the human mind and body is so great that he regards resentment as a cancer to the personality that is just as deadly as the physical disease. Dr. Stringham said we should ask our self if we are a resent-er. Do we want to get even with someone? Or does thoughts of a past event make us boil inside? If it does, then we resent and we are a resent-er!

A few years ago, a person recounted to me what she thought was an injustice done her by her mother, now long gone, regarding another sister when they were both small children. As she talked, tears ran down her face as obviously she was feeling the same emotion (hurt) she had felt previously. I sat there amazed as the incident had occurred over sixty years prior to that time. I doubt that this person even realized that she was harboring resentment.

How do we get rid of resentment? Pray for the person whom we resent, be especially nice to them; and, last, ask God and keep asking God to take our resentment away until it is gone. How should we pray for other persons, especially those we resent. Ephesians 1:17 says we should pray that they would have the spirit of wisdom and revelation in the knowledge of God, meaning come to know God or have a closer relationship with him.

Dr. Wayne Blankenship who was the pastor at the First Baptist Church in Weatherford, Texas where I was a member at that time preached a sermon one Sunday on Grace. I do not remember what he said, but from that sermon I came to understand what Grace really is. Basically Grace is a quality that enables God to forgive the undeserving. When we ask God for this quality called Grace, we, too, can look beyond the malice, prejudices, and injustices done to us and extend forgiveness to those who have done nothing to deserve it. In this way, we can rid our self of resentment.

3. **When do we forgive?** Now, daily, hourly, and minutely. We are so angered, hurt, or bitter at times that we do not forgive. We may feel that we can forgive tomorrow or next week, or sometime in the future; but what if we suddenly became ill and died or were killed in an accident? We would stand before God with an unclean heart, unforgiven, because we hold unforgiveness in our own heart.

4. **How do we forgive?** By practicing the Secret of the Will. I learned this secret from Catherine Marshall's book **Beyond Ourselves.**[6] This is what she said:

> *"The secret is simply this: that the Christian life must be lived in the will, not in the emotions; that God regards the*

*decisions and choices of a man's will as the decisions and choices of the man himself—no matter how contrary his emotions may be. Moreover, when this principle is applied, the emotions must always capitulate to the will."*

Our emotions prevent us from forgiving because we do not feel like forgiving, but we can still forgive by this act of will. To rid our self of every unforgiveness in our heart, every time an injustice, hurt, or act held against someone arises in our thoughts, we should say, "Lord, I forgive." And mean it! Probably it will be some time before we realize these injustices do not keep cropping up in our thoughts; and even if they do, they no longer cause feelings of anger, hurt, or bitterness. Resentment dissolves. Grudges disappear. The desire for revenge evaporates. Consider what has been said by others: That every moment we allow our self to be unhappy because of what someone else has done is a moment of happiness we could have had that is lost to us forever.

We can thankfully leave vengeance to God. *Vengeance is mine. I will repay; saith the Lord (Romans 12:19 KJV).* This should be a tremendous relief. Now we do not have to worry about whether that person gets his just deserts or whether we have dealt fairly and justly with the situation. We as mere human mortals cannot know what makes another person act as they do, but God knows all and is totally fair and just. Therefore, the Law of Retribution never fails. It is always an active force. What is this Law of Retribution? It means that for every wrongdoing, act or word, God, in his timing, will punish!

5. **The rewards of Forgiveness:** The rewards of forgiving are myriad. When we forgive, we then acquire the capacity to pray for those who abuse, persecute, and spitefully use us with some of the same compassion that Christ had as he looked down upon those who persecuted him. Even hanging on the cross in his own physical agony, seeing the reality of their true condition, separation from God, the most pitiful of all human conditions, he said, *"Father, forgive them; for they know not what they do" (Luke 23:34 KJV).*

Wanda said, "Oh, he knew what he was doing." Yes, he knew and they knew what they were doing to the same extent that others know what they are doing when they inflict injustices upon us, but they knew not (did not understand) that what they were doing separated them from

God; therefore, when someone does us an injustice, we should see their separation from God and pray for them just as Christ did.

The solution to much unhappiness and many of life's problems is forgiving. When we forgive, God forgives. When God forgives, we have a clean heart. We feel good about our self. Then instead of wasting our life being unhappy or miserable because of what someone else has done, or even perhaps something we may have done, something that cannot be changed, the past can be put behind and we can concentrate on the future, go forward. Forgiving leads to true happiness, and this happiness shines from our inner being for all to see. The greatest gift we can give to our loved ones, family, friends, and others is to teach them **The Value of Forgiving**.

In the up's and down's of life, psychologists tell us that it is not the exciting times that cause trouble. It is the inability to accept and deal constructively (be happy) with the boredom and dullness of routine everyday life, responsibilities, and the mundane. The reasons for unhappiness are myriad, but basically there are three kinds:

(1) Unhappiness brought on by tragedy, perhaps a death or illness or even just the normal storms of life which cause grief for a normal length of time; however, if we hold onto this type of grief and unhappiness, it becomes unhealthy.
(2) The most common kind of unhappiness is chronic unhappiness which usually stems from a trapped feeling of being in a situation, not to our liking, where there seems no hope of change. Most situations, especially serious ones, cannot be changed overnight, but they can by working on them over a period of time. Sadly, some situations can never be changed because of the circumstances such as being permanently disabled or occasionally because a new perspective cannot be comprehended. Being presented with a problem, I have offered suggestions which would have been a solution to the problem only to have that person say, "That won't work."

And

(3) unhappiness caused by one thinking they are unhappy. Those who seemingly have many of the blessings of life but continually harp

on what they don't have and consequently think of all kinds of reasons for being unhappy.

Life is spent like money in many ways. Suddenly we are old and if every phase is void of happiness, it is lost in a misspent life being unhappy. If you want to do something, do it now if possible, reprogram, work on working it in. Life can be exciting. Some put off doing what they really want to do until they retire or until this or that happens only to find that when that time comes, health fails or a spouse dies; and they never get to do all those things they wanted to do.

There are phases in the lives of children as they pass from one growth stage to the next, but adulthood is also a series of phases. Whether this fact is accepted affects our whole life. We start as children with all the excitement of growing up, become a single adult, get married, have children, children grow up and leave home, we retire and life changes again and again. Adjustments are required for each new change. If the capability is not acquired to enjoy and make the most of each new phase, it is spent waiting for the next phase that is supposed to bring happiness but never does because each phase has its own adjustments, challenges, problems, heartaches and tragedies along the way.

Parents become unhappy because they do not want to let go of their children and never get over their desire to give to them. The generations of today mostly want to start out with what it took parents thirty or forty years to acquire through work, struggle, and sacrifice. What is even worse, parents want them to have what they have also. They don't want them to go through the same hard struggles they did, not realizing that it is in the struggle that we grow in maturity; in our failures that we acquire the capacity to appreciate our successes, and through our defeats that we experience the true joy of victory when we succeed.

What is termed as wonderful opportunities for children provided by parents on what is commonly called a silver platter could never mean as much to children as the same opportunities meant to parents who struggled to achieve a goal because the children didn't spend all those years struggling; therefore, they have not acquired the capacity to appreciate. But when they have finally achieved their own goals in life (not goals we set for them) through their own struggles, hard work, sacrifice, failures and defeats, then they too will have acquired this same sense of appreciation that we have.

I once had a literature teacher in high school whom I loved very much, but now have even forgotten her name. In class one day, she quoted this quotation by some famous poet: *"Happy is the man who lays down to sleep with nothing to regret."* I do not know why this quotation stuck so firmly in my mind all through the years and wondered for a long time why this was such a great quotation. Now, more than fifty years later, I know the meaning of that quotation. Regret prevents us from being happy; therefore, we should work toward not doing something we will regret later.

If I have learned anything at all about how to find happiness, it is by understanding and accepting the following three things:

(1) We have only what we have today; there is no guarantee for tomorrow, even of life. All things are temporary. Life is temporary. Marriages are temporary (terminated either by death or divorce). Material possessions are temporary. Even the world is temporary (2 Peter 3:10).
(2) Constant excitement is not a prerequisite for happiness. Happiness means many things to different people. Happiness may mean the simple things like just coming home after a hard day to rest, spend time with the family and quietly watch television, or read.
(3) Life is too short to spend it being unhappy. If we could ask God for one thing and have it what would we ask for: Wealth, power, position, prestige? No. The one thing most of us want is happiness.

Ultimate true happiness then can be achieved by striving to become the kind of person God wants us to be and living a life centered on God. How? Have you tried prayer?

# Chapter 2

## HAVE YOU TRIED PRAYER

Prayer, like an electric cord, is our power line to God. Amazing! The power of prayer is illimitable in our lives if we can but learn how to utilize it. Most of us have been taught how to pray some kind of prayer, but to **learn how to pray effectively** is a process of learning just like everything else.

This process of learning began for me a few years after suffering through the heartache of a broken marriage and the seemingly endless frustrations of despair, guilt, and what seemed to be unsolvable problems. There were the demands imposed upon me in struggling to maintain a home and earn enough money to provide just for physical necessities and coping with the residual emotional needs of a very upset little boy as well as myself. I could endure the hardship for myself, but it was the welfare of my son that I agonized over. My agony was intensified by the reason for the breakup of my marriage—my husband was mentally ill. His years of covering up disintegrated exposing his mental condition. What could no longer be denied was acknowledged. As he sat and told me of the years of deceit, lies, and immorality, the shock, hurt, humiliation, and fear I experienced was indescribable.

After ten years of endless frustration, not knowing what the problem was but trying to cope with a person who at times was a very giving, loving, and rational human being while at others was devious, grossly selfish, and totally unreasonable, I could endure no more. I sat and cried and simply said, "This is the end." But even in my own pain, I realized that when he saw how badly he had hurt me, he was just as hurt as I was and did not understand his own behavior any more than I did. We sat, two broken-hearted people, and cried together.

Those next few years, even though it did not show on the surface, I was truly one of the walking wounded. At that time, I had not learned how to deal constructively with the storms of life. I reacted instead of acting. Because there was no money left after all the bills had been paid, just surviving was difficult that first year. My sister Fay let me move in with her until I could find a job and reestablish a home for myself and my son. This was a hardship on her as well as the rest of her family. It took months just to find a job and get settled, and then my salary was so small there were times when there was hardly enough money for food. My little son kept wanting to go home to the home he knew; he wanted his daddy.

My husband committed himself into a state-supported hospital where psychiatric treatment was available to those who were unable to afford private psychiatric help. He was assigned to a Dr. Winston Martin. His condition was diagnosed as acute schizophrenia which is a deterioration of the human personality. In his case, resulting from a deep-seated guilt complex stemming from early childhood because **he thought** his parents did not love him; therefore, if they did not love him, it was his fault. Dr. Martin explained that his behavior patterns reflected actions that required condemnation as self-punishment in an effort to rid himself of his feelings of guilt.

I visited Dr. Martin on two or three occasions at his request and corresponded to discuss my husband's condition and progress. I shall always be eternally grateful to Dr. Martin. Even though at that time I did not fully understand all that he was explaining to me, what he said helped, in later years, to remove some of the confusion resulting from my lack of knowledge of mental illness. When Dr. Martin was informed that it was my intention to put my husband legally and physically out of my life and the life of my son, he asked me to wait in the hope that this would expedite therapy, and so I waited—and waited—and waited with my life on hold. It was three years before his condition was diagnosed "in social remission" which means that he was able to cope in society, if too much stress was not imposed upon him. During those years, I learned from Dr. Martin and other sources some rather interesting and important facts about mental illness that helped to constructively rebuild my own life:

(1) That while physical insanity can be hereditary, mental illness of the emotions and personality are usually the result of environmental factors.
(2) That while some schizophrenia is caused by a lack of love and treatment of that individual, much schizophrenia is caused not because a person was not loved but because **he thought** he was not loved as a child.
(3) That mental illness manifests itself in varying degrees and many behavior patterns.
(4) That guilt and fear deteriorate the human personality more rapidly than any other thing.

And

(5) that because there is no cure for the mentally ill, psychiatrists work toward goals of improvement rather than curing of the disease.

And all during this time, I cried out to God, Why? Why? Why? Why did you let this happen to me? I didn't do anything to deserve this. Worst of all, I could find no right solutions to the problems confronting me. I cried a million tears; I would have cried a million more if it would have helped, but tears do not remove the stark reality of mental illness, nor repair a marriage irrevocably damaged, nor heal a broken heart. After three years of agonizing indecision, I got a divorce in an attempt to put the past behind and go forward with my own life. But divorce does not solve all problems; it merely exchanges one set for another in some cases, especially when children are involved.

The next few years were busy ones. I attained a measure of financial security through employment with the Department of Army and purchased a small older home. My son was busy in school, and we were both involved in church activities. We enjoyed the benefits of living next door to my sister and her family and being included in holiday gatherings and summers spent in outings at the lake. Even though those were lonely years, they were also happy ones with memories that we both look back on and treasure. My sister had seven grandchildren, and my son became what amounted to the eighth, as he was only a year-and-a-half older than her oldest grandchild.

But all was not smooth sailing. There were still a lot of residual problems dealing with my former husband's mental illness in connection with our son. After my son's infrequent visits with his father, usually months later, in times of stress, resentment erupted in open hostility and rebellion toward his mother—me! His father never criticized me directly but because of his impaired mental capacity, it was obvious that insidious innuendoes were at the root of this resentment, caused by his separation from his father, as it all poured out: "Daddy said . . . . Daddy said . . . . Daddy said that he would like for us to live with him, but you won't do it. Daddy said he would come live with us, but you won't let him. Daddy said he did some things he shouldn't have, but it was because you were too good to him. Et cetera, et cetera! But his father never went on to explain that he was ill and couldn't handle the responsibility or stress that a normal marriage relationship imposed upon him; therefore, it's mother's fault. It's mother's fault that you can't live with daddy.

It is impossible for a child, or even an adult, to understand the logic of the mentally ill. They never accept the responsibility for their own actions; therefore, they must point out by one means or another that whatever they do is someone else's fault. Sadly, the many admirable qualities his father had, overshadowed by his illness, could only be maintained for short periods of time. Dr. Martin's advice that the child, when he was small, be told his father had problems, sadly, was ignored through another poor choice on my part. The child was not told because I thought it would adversely affect him to know his father was mentally ill; but had I followed this good doctor's advice, the child could have been spared all the suffering he endured through those growing-up years because of a lack of understanding.

In subsequent years, I wished many times that I had put my husband legally and physically out of my life and the life of my son when the child was a baby instead of following the advice of Dr. Martin and allowing his father to continue seeing him, thereby disrupting our lives. I lived in absolute terror that my son, too, would become mentally ill from all the turmoil created by his father. When my son was in his early teens, it became obvious that telling the child about his father's condition could no longer avoided; it had to be done.

Here was another valuable lesson: Even a small child can cope with the truth, no matter how bad it is, better than he can cope with a lack of understanding. Only then, looking back through the many years, could I see the wisdom of Dr. Martin's words in advising me not to prevent the child from seeing his father but to explain that his father had some problems because to my son, his father was wonderful. He was a vacation father who imposed no responsibilities or rules upon him, who for the short periods of time he was with him, played games, took him fishing, and other special places.

And yet another important lesson is this: Many problems cannot be solved because we are looking for the ideal (perfect) solution. But the ideal does not exist. If it did, we wouldn't have the problem in the first place. So there is the ideal versus a workable solution. When we are willing to accept a workable solution, a situation can usually be improved, although the initial problem may not be solved completely. In such an extremely difficult situation, how could anyone make a child, even a teenager, understand mental illness without seeming to criticize? I couldn't explain it, nor even understand it myself. The only sensible solution was to have an extremely competent person do it, so I contacted a Christian counseling center and requested the name of a reputable psychiatrist in that area. They furnished three names.

Again, it is astounding how God guides and directs us. I decided on the last name on the list, Dr. James Shackelford. But being fearful of choosing the wrong one, I called the first name on the list for an appointment, only to be told that he did not treat children. Likewise, the second name on the list was contacted, but he was not accepting any new patients. So Dr. Shackelford, the last name on the list and the one originally selected, was called for an appointment.

I shall never forget that first interview. How could I ever explain my husband's condition to make even this psychiatrist understand enough so he could explain to the child the complexities of mental disease of a patient he had never seen? I asked him if he treated children, and he did. He then asked about my health and job; I told him I was fine. He asked if the child had problems with grades in school or at home; I told him he was doing fine. Why then was I here? After several disjointed, almost incoherent statements on my part trying to explain the father's mental illness and why I wanted to bring the child to him, he suddenly exclaimed, "Oh, you want me to explain to the child so he can understand his father's condition!" "Yes, yes," I said, "that is why I am here."

I then sat and listened in complete astonishment as he related how he had been working at the same hospital where my husband had been a patient and in all probability had been one of his treating psychiatrists; was very familiar with his type of illness, and would have no problem making the child understand. He did make the child understand which alleviated many future problems. This kind and brilliant doctor also assured and reassured me that my fears were groundless; that my son would not become mentally ill like his father. Coincidence? I cannot believe it was. To me, it was a miracle! Nobody but God could bring together such isolated events with such perfect timing:

(1) The doctor working for years in that particular hospital, treating my husband.
(2) Relocating all the way across the State of Texas to Fort Worth close to my area.
(3) Being brilliant and thoroughly competent with a unique and uncanny ability to grasp the fundamentals of a situation with only meager facts.

And,

(4) being available at the exact time I contacted the counseling center.

Years later, it was my habit to spend the time commuting to and from work in prayer. It was a nice peaceful drive on a country highway. During one of these morning drives I was explaining to God my actions when suddenly a letter that I had written to Dr. Martin flashed in front of me. I remembered writing to Dr. Martin, in response to his inquiry as to whether or not a reconciliation with my then husband was possible, in which I thanked him for his time and efforts, and then ended this letter with: "All the things you have explained to me have provided a reason for my husband's behavior, but it does not take away the pain nor does it provide an excuse for such behavior—because there is none."

**"Because there is none!"** That phrase from my own letter stood before my eyes in bold black letters, as if it were written on the windshield. It occurred to me that all these things I was explaining to God were reasons for my behavior, not excuses. I do not even remember what that behavior was that I was trying to justify, probably some unkind thing I had said. Suddenly, I realized that I stood before God guilty for any unacceptable thought or act. I had no excuse—because there is none! It was at that moment that I believe I understood the true meaning of forgiveness and how prayer can affect us. We do not forgive others because they deserve forgiveness; we forgive them because God has forgiven us. It was at this time also that I believe the healing process of my inner being began, freeing me from resentment, bitterness, unforgiveness, and anger—anger at my husband for inflicting so much needless pain and unhappiness into my life, anger at myself for having placed myself in a position to be subjected to such unhappiness, and, yes, even anger at God for letting it happen.

And it was at this time, too, that God answered my questions of long ago: Why? Why? Why? Why did you let this happen to me? I didn't do anything to deserve this. And God's answer was, "Yes, you did. You saw the signs, yet you ignored them and went ahead with the marriage; and even though you could do nothing to change the course of events (your husband's deteriorating mental illness) after having made that choice, once that choice was made, the results (heartache) were inevitable." In other words, you unwittingly brought all this upon yourself. You should blame no one but yourself for your own unhappiness.

God answers prayer at a point when we can accept and understand. I came to understand then that when we make poor choices, we do literally become the victims of our own poor judgment. And with this understanding, I had to accept the responsibility for those choices. The anger began to dissolve. Obviously, God was not at fault. Obviously, too, my anger at my husband was unjustified as I finally was able to comprehend what Dr. Martin had explained: That the mentally ill have no control over their own actions. Like any disease, the victim is not at fault or has any control over his own illness. This does not excuse their behavior, but it is for God to deal with them. Obviously, the anger at myself was unjustified also because the average person, which I certainly was, cannot recognize or cope intelligently with mental illness. I lacked the age, wisdom, knowledge, education, experience and maturity to deal constructively with situations I had been confronted with.

It was also during this time of growing in spiritual maturity that I was reading one of Dr. Peale's many books in which he referred to one of his small booklets called **Thought Conditioners**[7] that can be ordered free from the Peale Center at Pawling, New York 12464 in which he said this booklet could change anyone's life. I thought—if anyone's life needs changing, certainly it is mine. I immediately ordered it, and it eventually came. I read it—but could not see anything extraordinarily great about it. After all, it was just a booklet containing some Scriptures with explanations outlining a concept that anyone can change their life by changing their thoughts. Dr. Peale said that just as an air conditioner keeps the air in a room clean and healthy, through a displacement process of removing unhealthy thoughts from the mind and replacing them with creative spiritual passages from the

Bible, healthy thoughts can be placed in the mind that would revolutionize one's whole personality, thereby changing their life.

At that time, I could not grasp the fundamental concept that he was teaching. I just could not visualize life being changed without the changing of circumstances, and so Thought Conditioners were set aside. This little booklet laid by my favorite chair week after week, for eight months—I counted them. Yet, I kept coming back to this little booklet. If he said it was so, it must be so.

Who can say at what point in time or who finally touches us individually that brings about comprehension. I believe it is a combination of many because it was some months later when one of my dearest friends, the late Dow Jordan, loaned me her copy of Catherine Marshall's book **Beyond Ourselves** that I began to understand the key to this concept. Mrs. Marshall outlined in minute detail specifically **how** to enter into a relationship with God in chapter 3; **how** to find God's will and **the Secret of the Will** in chapter 4; the importance of forgiveness in chapter 8, **Ego-slaying** in chapter 12; and **The Prayer that Helps Your Dreams Come True** in chapter 11. I loved that, especially the part about making dreams come true as I certainly had many, many dreams that had not come true. She listed seven steps by which to test our prayers to know whether what we are asking for is possible through the Dreaming Prayer:

(1) Whether our dream fulfills the talents, temperament, and emotional needs that God himself planted in us.
(2) Does our dream involve hurting another human being or taking anything or any person from someone else? If it does, that is not God's will for us.
(3) Do we want our dream with our whole heart?
(4) Are we willing to wait patiently for God to bring this dream into being?
(5) Are we dreaming big? The bigger the dreams are and the more people benefited by them, the greater God's blessings will be on our dream.
(6) Are we willing to hand our dream over to God and leave it with him?
(7) And are we willing to make all our relationships right with other people? To hold grudges, resentments, and bitterness—no matter how justified they are—wrong emotions such as these cut us off from God.

I decided to practice **The Secret of the Will** as outlined in Chapter 4 and **Ego-Slaying** as outlined in Chapter 12. Mrs. Marshall emphasized that the **Secret of the Will** is that the Christian life must be lived in the will, not the emotion, and **Ego-Slaying** means that it is not enough to commit only part of our life to God. We must commit total self. Mrs. Marshall advised that unless we are serious about acquiring a closer relationship with God, we should not make this total commitment. If we hold on to any little thing that we delude our self into thinking that we are not doing wrong or are ashamed of, it will surface and we will be required to acknowledge it, deal with it, and put it out of our life.

This has proved to be true over and over; and since the time that I made this total commitment to God and put into practice the concepts of the dreaming prayer, wonderful things have never stopped happening. Instead of agonizing over problem after problem and saying, "Lord, nothing is happening; won't you do something," I've had to say, "Lord, would you please slow down so I can catch up!" Did I stop at that point learning, praying, trying to grow and committing my life to God? No! That was just the beginning.

In John Bisagno's book **The Power of Positive Praying**,[8] he says that one of the reasons for unanswered prayers is because the big "if" is put before prayers by saying "if" this be your will, grant this prayer. When, in reality, God's will should first be determined and then ask God for it. How then is God's will to be determined? There are two kinds of God's will:

(1) His set or determined will, meaning things set by God that are beyond human control or ability to change such as birth, parents, brothers, sisters, sex, genetic features, color of hair and eyes, race, and death.
(2) His permissive will, meaning he wants us to live his way but will not force us, and this is divided into two categories:

   (a) That which is outlined in his laws.
   (b) That which we must find step-by-step in daily life such as which job to choose, where to live, choosing a mate, life-style, et cetera.

It is not difficult to find out what God's will is in his laws. These are outlined in specific codes of behavior in the Ten Commandments, and there are even more specific instructions in the Bible:

*(3, 4) For God wants you to be holy and pure, and to keep clear of all sexual sin so that each of you will marry in holiness and honor—(5) not in lustful passion as the heathen do, in their ignorance of God and his ways. (6) And this also is God's will: That you never cheat in this matter by taking another man's wife, because the Lord will punish you terribly for this, as we have solemnly told you before (1 Thessalonians 4:3-6 LB).*

God's will is further outlined:

*(14) Dear brothers, warn those who are lazy; comfort those who are frightened; take tender care of those who are weak; and be patient with everyone. (15) See that no one pays back evil for evil, but always try to do good to each other and to everyone else. (16) Always be joyful. (17) Always keep on praying. (18) No matter what happens, always be thankful for this is God's will for you who belong to Christ Jesus (1 Thessalonians 5:14-18 LB).*

It is knowing exactly what God's will is for daily life that is the most difficult to discern. Most of the time we don't even ask God; we just do what we want to. But when genuinely seeking God's will, keep in mind Charles Allens book **All things are Possible Through Prayer**[9] in which he says, "Be careful what you pray for, you might get it." Over and over, this has also proved to be true. I have learned there is a price to pay for everything. Do we want to sacrifice, work and put forth the effort to bring our requests into being. Back in the early 1970s, I once told my friend Melanie Stringer that if I ask God for something, he would probably give it to me; but I was not sure that I wanted to go through what it would take to get it.

Another way of finding God's will is by following principles others have used. Ruth Stafford Peale wrote a booklet called **This Thing Called Guidance**[10] in which she said that if a door has closed for no apparent reason or through no fault of our own, God is trying to guide us to another door, one that is even better than the one we want. In the works of Dr. Peale, he said that a vision of our innermost desires should be held up to God in prayer. In one of Dr. Peale's printed sermons **Insight That Sees Through**

**Confusion,**[11] he tells about the famous Gladys Aylward who based her whole life on God's guidance. She used five ways of finding God's will:

(1) A strong inner conviction.
(2) The opening of doors.
(3) The closing of doors.
(4) Hearing the voice of God.
(5) And last, God's Word in the Bible.

By following all these principles and fundamental truths for finding God's will, do I get everything I want or pray for? No, but there have been astounding results again and again. Disappointments are short-lived because without a doubt that was not what God wanted for me or what was best. Finally, I was able to grasp the fundamental concept that one's life can indeed be changed by changing our thoughts. The paradox of this is that once the thoughts begin to change, the circumstances also change, just as Dr. Peale said. I do not understand it; I just know how my life changed because of it.

I was morosely watching television one Sunday afternoon deploring my work situation at the Primary Helicopter Training Center at Fort Wolters, Texas where I was employed in the Transportation Division. My job had become very routine. Suddenly there flashed on the screen, The Exciting Challenge of Court Reporting. A new court reporting college was now open in my area. Being a court reporter was something I had always been profoundly interested in as a career, not only because of its monetary potential but because it is such an interesting profession. However, there had been no hope whatsoever of attaining such a goal. Immediately, I sent off for information and was disappointed to find that it cost several thousand dollars just for tuition alone; dollars I didn't have.

Occasionally year after year passes with only seemingly small insignificant changes in our life, and then there are drastic changes. Suddenly, it was announced that Fort Wolters was closing and all positions would be abolished. With this announcement came personnel options. Those unable to be reassigned because of inability to relocate would be entitled to severance pay. This became an opportunity to enroll in the full-time study course at the court reporting college although finances would be drastically limited to the sacrificial point. There was no income during that time other than the severance pay and a very small savings. After fourteen months of hard grueling study, I graduated and became a certified court reporter. It was a great day! God had provided.

Now came the next difficult step: Finding employment for a beginner in an area saturated with reporters because of the court reporting college. While I continued attending the college from which I had graduated in an effort to increase my proficiency, a notice appeared on the bulletin board for a court in Arkansas. My application was mailed to the newly elected Circuit Judge Henry Wilkinson, and he hired me in May of 1978. I was to begin work on January 1, 1979.

From the moment I moved to Arkansas, I loved it. I missed my family, but I loved the work, and I loved working for Judge Wilkinson. I continued working in this particular court for sixteen years until both the judge and I retired on January 1, 1995. Was there any doubt that the Lord had truly led me to this particular court? No! I never had to worry about whether this was right or this was where God wanted me to be. There had been no courts available anywhere near my area in the State of Texas. I sent out numerous resumes with no results. But not too many months after I had accepted the position in Arkansas several courts in Texas became available, even the one in the town in which I lived. Did I apply for any of them? No. I had already accepted the position in Arkansas, and I had told the judge I would be there.

The proof of whether this court had been the right one for me was further substantiated after I retired. Once when the judge and I were discussing how much I had enjoyed working for him all those years, I told him about all the jobs I had applied for but there were just no courts available in my area until after he had hired me. He then related that he had received virtually no applications except mine in response to his notice for a reporter until after he had hired me, and then they just came pouring in. And, he said, "I had to tell them that the position had already been filled." Was all this another coincidence? I cannot think so!

Thinking back on the requirements in Mrs. Marshal's dreaming prayer, I discovered that court reporting truly fulfilled my talents and suited my particular temperament and emotional needs. It did not involve taking anything from anyone else. I certainly did want it with my whole heart. I didn't wait patiently on God, but he fulfilled my dream anyway, in his time, not mine. I left my dream with God, and he brought it into being. Never again will I suffer acute disappointment. I will unfailingly know that if a prayer is not granted or a door closes, God is guiding me to something better.

What I learned through these many years from the works of all these great people about how life can be changed and the solution to many of life's problems can be found through prayer, their teachings have merged into five major points:

(1) Learn to pray effectively by following the guidelines set out by others who lived successful lives through prayer.
(2) Replace unhealthy (bad) thoughts with healthy (good) ones.
(3) Total commitment to God.
(4) Govern one's life through the will, not the emotions.
(5) Center thoughts on God. Concentrate not on the problem but center thoughts on God's awesome greatness, power, goodness and glory.

Through prayer and practicing these principles, God changed my life. He can do the same for you:

# Chapter 3

## DON'T CRY FOR ME

It has been said that a broken marriage can be compared to a beautiful new schooner in all its shinning glory sailing away with its white sails flying high toward an exciting adventure on an uncharted course, but is ill-prepared for the long voyage ahead. And as it continues on its journey mercilessly beat and battered by the storms of life, arrives not at its intended destination, but washed ashore a hopeless wreckage beyond repair.

This is the condition in which I found my marriage during the early 1960s, a hopeless wreckage beyond repair. God's ideal for a man and woman joined together in the bonds of holy matrimony has always been a life-long commitment and life together. I did not want to depart from God's teachings; therefore, there seemed to be no solutions to the heartbreaking problems confronting me. Thus, it was in my own search through Biblical teachings for solutions on how to deal with a broken marriage that I learned many things about the causes of divorce and what God says on the subject in the Bible.

As a Christian, when confronted with decisions concerning a divorce, it is difficult to find solutions because of the complexities involved in each individual situation and because of controversial teachings in churches, but there is much one can learn on the subject of marriage, divorce, and remarriage from a Biblical standpoint:

**First,** a marriage is a life-long commitment combined with a legal binding contract. This is God's ideal.

**Second**, there are two ways by which a marriage can be terminated, and that is by (1) death and (2) by a legal action.

And, **third,** the termination of any marriage is the result of sin. When death occurs in a marriage, the marriage is terminated. Death became the result of sin with the Fall of Man; therefore, the marriage is terminated as a result of sin being in the world. A marriage that is terminated by a legal action, divorce, is the result of sin, rather than the divorce itself being the sin. By the time a situation becomes so intolerable that a divorce is inevitable, multitudes of sins have usually been committed by one or both parties.

God's ideal for man also was to live in a sin-free world without unhappiness, disease, and death. But since the Fall of Man, the ideal does not exist, and man has since been faced with the reality of coping with that which is not ideal. Most persons accept the fact that man now lives in a state less than God's ideal; yet, many of those same persons will not accept or make any effort to understand that it is because man is thrust into this less than idyllic state that society has become plagued with yet another disease called divorce which, according to statistics, has reached epidemic proportions. Therefore, it is one of life's situations that must be dealt with, hopefully in a constructive manner.

The causes of divorce are myriad: Mental illnesses of varying degrees, alcoholism, drug addiction, poor judgment, poor money management, immaturity, immorality, and physical abuse ranking high among them. But regardless of the cause, the results are the same. When you see divorce, you see tragedy, broken hearts, and shattered lives.

Excluding the more drastic causes, it becomes obvious through working with singles that one of the main causes of divorce is resentment. Astounding? Yes. Instead of appreciating and being thankful for any admirable qualities of one's mate, petty issues are blown all out of proportion. Everyone resents things from time to time, but for those persons who practice holding resentments in their heart, resentments build and build. Constant harping and petty criticisms become persistent nagging and eventually ill will toward the one resented, damaging and in some cases eventually destroying what could be an otherwise loving relationship.

Another common cause for divorce is that those contemplating marriage do not look at the true qualities of character of their would-be future mate. Physical attraction, lack of availability of suitable mates, and sheer loneliness dominates choices of mates rather than looking at character and personality traits. Whatever faults they see in the other are ignored. Even worse, they use the rationalization that I will change them or one changes after marriage, not realizing that one does not necessarily change for the better in marriage.

In working with singles over the years and seeing almost as many divorces among second and third marriages as there is among first marriages, it becomes apparent that regardless of age, whether in youth or older age, the propensity for error never diminishes. However, the fact can never be ignored that many put their best foot forward, and the old adage "what you see is what you get" cannot be applied because what you got wasn't what you saw.

What then is the criteria for choosing a mate to insure a happy and lasting marriage? Instead of relying mainly on physical attraction, look at the potential mate's interests. Do they like the same things you do, not just the big things but the small things also. Check their present habits and lifestyle keeping in mind that this is what you will be living with day in and day out, week after week, year after year. Consider the following common complaints:

(1) Enjoying the same kind of televisions programs, entertainment, foods, et cetera—
(2) If she is not a good housekeeper now, she won't be after you are married—
(3) If he is untidy, he will be untidy after you are married and have to be picked up after—
(4) If one likes to throw away, and the other insists on keeping every piece of clutter—
(5) If one is an avid sports fan and monopolizes the television and you are bored to death with sports—
(6) If one likes to party all the time and the other is a homebody and would rather putter around the house—
(7) If one likes to travel and the other would rather quietly stay at home—
(8) If one is conservative in management of finances and the other is a spendthrift or lives for the minute spending more than they can afford—
(9) If one has to do all the work around the house and the other doesn't pitch in—

(10) Lack of support and cooperation to the demands of the other's interests, ambitions or employment—
(11) And on and on—

All differences difficult to tolerate create dissention, tension, resentment, anger, and eventually, unfortunately and unhappily, in some cases the breakup of a marriage. Romantic illusions quickly fade after marriage for those not prepared for the reality of the responsibilities involved. When two people merge their life, there are always innumerable differences that have to be reconciled. Much cooperation and tolerance is required as separate jobs are to be maintained, money managed, children cared for, homes organized in which somebody has to wash piles of dirty laundry, cook, do mountains of dishes, and cleaning, et cetera.

Love between the sexes is such a fragile thing. It's like a delicate flower. If we water and treat a flower with tender loving care, it grows and blooms profusely; but if we walk out the door and step on it every day, it soon withers and dies. So it is with love. God's admonition to the husband is to nourish and cherish his wife, and the wife is to respect her husband. Harsh thoughtless unkind words that can never be recalled, unkind thoughtless actions, self-centeredness, selfishness, resentments, grudges, and lack of consideration on the part of either husband or wife wither love and keep it from growing and blooming, and everyone loses.

The question is: Do I really love this person? And contrary to popular opinion, love can be measured. It is measured by how we treat someone. If I have learned anything at all through these experiences, it is this: If we truly love someone, we do not want to say or do anything to hurt them. I never really understood this kind of love until I had my son Mark. Regardless of what he does, I will never want to hurt him. In the realities of life between husband and wife, there are always likes, dislikes, irritations, resentments, and anger. But if we truly love someone, we can set aside these things and treat the other person in a loving manner.

In watching TV recently where a tornado had demolished a fifteen-mile wide path, a surviving victim, his wife and baby were hurtled 300 feet. His wife had held on to the baby until she was knocked unconscious. When she woke up the baby was gone. The man finally found his wife as she frantically searched for the baby. A rescue worker looking through some scattered debris saw a tiny leg sticking out of the mud and pulled the baby out and frantically cleaned the mud out of its nose and mouth. When finally the baby started to cry, the joy was indescribable. And the father, when reunited with his family and clutching the baby to him, said it all when he said: **"When you love someone, hold on to them and treasure them; God gives them to us and he allows them to be taken away, so we never know now long we will have them."**

How do you know you are really in love? Take the test. Honestly analyze and write down all good qualities and all faults of a potential partner. If the faults outweigh the good qualities, better do some serious reconsidering. However, we cannot discount that special quality that someone has that attracts one to another, that no one else can see. I call it the undefined quality. This is the quality that creates the no-fault person, just like no-fault insurance. My delightful son proved there is just such a person.

Just prior to the turmoil of the teens which began with an almost angelic agreeable ten-year-old which I have since called the golden year, we went through the eleven and twelve-year-old stage. Beginning the teens, I wondered why all the fuss about the terrible teens. Then one week when my son was about thirteen-and-a-half, every time I opened my mouth, in that tone of voice that a parent usually uses to patiently explain something to a small child, he said, "Mother, are you retarded or something!" I knew the terrible teens had begun.

At seventeen the question was, "Mother, are you getting senile?" And then progressing to the old age of eighteen with increased wisdom, while correcting my careful driving when I was bringing him home from the hospital after having some surgery on his hand, I was advised, "Mother, what you really need is a head transplant!" But finally his mother began to grow up, and he could see the wisdom of her teachings to some small extent and thankfully progressed to a mature young man of nineteen.

It was at this time in his first year in college that he became engaged to a beautiful young lady. He was truly in love; to him she was perfect. They dated. They broke up. He would start dating someone else. She would call or write. He would drop whomever he was dating and go back to her. Being a concerned and helpful parent, I asked him one day while discussing his engagement to take an unsolicited test I had received through the mail entitled, **How Do You Know You're in Love?**[12] Looking at me with those big brown eyes and in a matter-of-fact tone (to humor his mother), he said, "Okay, mother! What do I do?" I told him to list all her good qualities, and he did. Then I told him to list all her faults, to which he promptly replied, "Oh, that's easy, mother, she doesn't have any!" To him, she truly was a no-fault person.

Her name was Angela, but the angelic qualities he saw in her did not exist. She broke his heart! The engagement was broken with the understanding that they would date until problems could be resolved. He went to pick her up one night for a date and came home a couple of hours later obviously stunned saying only that she was married. When he arrived to pick her up she introduced her new husband to him; no call; no letter; no warning; just, "I'm married. This is my husband."

He never mentioned her name again. Suffering in silence, he didn't even date for over a year. I think that the most difficult part in being a parent is having to watch one's child suffer and being helpless to alleviate that suffering. Years later, because he had not seriously considered marriage again, I asked him if it was because of his experience with Angela. He said, "No, I can see now that what happened was for the best. It would never have worked out." And I thanked God that he had been spared the tragedy of divorce.

Though we cannot ignore the many other heartbreaking causes of divorce, the fact remains that some divorces are caused because people change over the years as their tastes, ambitions, and goals in life change and they find they have little or nothing in common with their mate. However, there is really **only one cause for divorce**. One or both partners do not follow God's outlines for a happy marriage nor put God first in their life.

What is God's guidance for a happy marriage? An outline is given for both a husband and a wife in the following Scriptures:

> *Wives, submit yourselves unto your own husbands, as unto the Lord. (Ephesians 5:22 KJV.)*

> *But I would have you know, that the head of every man is Christ; and the head of woman is the man; and the head of Christ is God (1 Corinthians 11:3 KJV.)*

> *(11) But remember that in God's plan men and women need each other. (12) For although the first woman came out of man, all men have been born from women ever since, and both men and women come from God their Creator (1 Corinthians 11:11-12 LB).*

> *Husbands, love your wives, even as Christ also loved the church, and gave himself for it. (Ephesians 5:25 KJV.)*

*(28) So ought men to love their wives as their own bodies. He that loveth his wife loveth himself. (29) For no man ever yet hated his own flesh; but nourisheth and cherisheth it, even as the Lord the church. (Ephesians 5:28-29 KJV.)*

All these Scriptures point to the same thing, mutual respect and love. The root word for submit in the above Scripture means to set in array under. Meaning that in God's hierarchy man is over woman, Christ is over man, and both are under God. This does not mean that wives are to cater to unreasonable whims of husbands but to treat them with respect. Husbands are to do the same, treating their wives as Christ treats them. Man and woman are equally to share in a relationship. Selfishness of one or both partners make this impossible. It is a proven fact that one partner alone cannot create a happy and successful marriage. In this day and age, because of societies growing instabilities, many husbands are too unstable to assume their proper role as heads and wives too immature to accept their own responsibilities.

So much is said about what wives are to do in the marriage relationship, but God gives man the greater responsibilities. Husbands are admonished to love their wives so much that they are even willing to die for them if necessary, just as Christ died for his church (Christians). Wives were given no such admonition. Wives were not admonished to even love their husbands (although that was desirable), but they were to honor and respect their husbands. Why?

These rules of behavior for husbands and wives were given during a time period when women were considered possessions and had no control over whom they married; therefore, they may not have loved their husbands so were admonished to respect them and their God-given position. It was their duty to do so in order to maintain a stable and peaceful home. On the other hand, husbands into whose care a woman was given was to love, protect, and care for her. What a tremendous responsibility God gave man!

And last, man as well as woman is given this admonition by God:

*Nevertheless let every one of you in particular so love his wife even as himself, and the wife see that she reverence her husband. (Ephesians 5:33 KJV.)*

If these laws of God were followed, there would be no need for anyone, man or woman, to even want a divorce. If a spouse will treat their mate with love and kindness, they will usually respond in like manner. But there are always exceptions. Sadly, no matter how well some are treated, they shamefully disregard the laws of God and treat a spouse unkindly with either words or deeds. Many also make the mistake of taking a spouse for granted or even worse using the old adage "you will always be there no matter what I do or how I treat you," and the damage becomes too great to repair. Many use this same old adage as a license to misuse or abuse many privileges in marriage instead of following God's laws and putting forth a genuine effort toward building a long-term stable marriage and happy relationship.

One summer when I was about sixteen years old and working at what is now called an old-fashioned soda fountain where light meals were served, a fairly young couple with two little boys, probably three and five, came every Saturday evening to eat. You could tell it was a special treat and they were strictly country; they had that healthy clean-scrubbed look. Though the wife was rotund and very plain, it was obvious that the husband loved her. One Saturday they came in and she being obviously upset did not order. As she sniffled quietly, the husband said over and over in a quiet pleading voice, "Better please eat something; better please eat something," as she shook her head. The unusual wording of his plea stuck in my mind all during the meal while the little boys were being fed and the husband ate trying to maintain some semblance of normalcy with two pair of little eyes turned upon them. Whatever daddy had done to cause mama to be hurt, daddy, obviously distressed because of that hurt, was trying in the only way he knew how to make amends. At the impressionable age of sixteen, that scene was indelibly imprinted on my mind as I thought—this is the kind of man I would like to marry.

It is the following Scriptures which probably are the most controversial because they address themselves not only to divorce but also to remarriage.

> *(10) And unto the married I command, yet not I but the Lord, let not the wife depart from her husband. (11) But and if she depart, let her remain unmarried, or be reconciled to her husband; and let not the husband put away his wife. (1 Corinthians 7:10-11 KJV.)*

> *(2) For the woman which has an husband is bound by the law to her husband so long as he liveth; but if the husband*

*be dead, she is loosed from the law of her husband. (3) So then if, while her husband liveth, she be married to another man, she shall be called an adulteress. But if her husband be dead, she is free from that law, so that she is no adulteress, though she be married to another man. (Romans 7:2-3 KJV.)*

*(31) The law of Moses says, "If anyone wants to be rid of his wife, he can divorce her merely by giving her a letter of dismissal. (32) But I say that a man who divorces his wife, except for fornication, causes her to commit adultery if she marries again. And he who marries her commits adultery." (Matthew 5:31:32 LB.)*

It is difficult to understand why an innocent party would be guilty of adultery if they remarried or the person who marries them commits adultery. Romans 7:3 states she shall be called an adulteress if she remarries possibly because the only legal reason for divorce was adultery, so she is presumed guilty of adultery. But Matthew 5:32 states she commits adultery if she remarries. Therefore, it is not clear whether the innocent party is actually guilty of adultery in God's eyes or just thought to be an adulteress since her husband divorced her.

In considering the meaning of these Scriptures, again it is important to remember that during this time period women were considered property and had no control over whom they married. If a wife found life intolerable with her husband she could leave, but she was to remain unmarried. Women could neither divorce their husbands nor support themselves. Therefore, if a woman left her husband she would in all probability have to return to him or return to her own family. The husband is given the admonition not to divorce his wife.

Jesus gives this further admonition concerning divorce and remarriage. This particular Scripture was written during a time period when wife swapping was prevalent. If a wife displeased her husband for any minor infraction, husbands were handing their wives a Bill of Divorcement and taking other wives. This was far short of God's ideal.

*(3) Some Pharisees came in to interview him, and tried to trap him into saying something that would ruin him. "Do you permit divorce?" they asked. (4) "Don't you read the*

> *Scriptures?" he replied. "'In them, it is written that at the beginning, God created man and woman, (5,6) and that a man should leave his father and mother, and be forever united to his wife. The two shall become one—no longer two, but one. And no man may divorce what God has joined together." (7) "Then why," they asked, "did Moses say a man may divorce his wife by merely writing her a letter of dismissal?" (8) Jesus replied, "Moses did that in recognition of your hard and evil hearts, but it was not what God had originally intended. (9) And I tell you this, that anyone who divorces his wife, except for fornication, and marries another, commits adultery." (Matthew 19:3-9 LB.)*

Those contemplating divorce should consider that it is abundantly clear from all these Scriptures that if anyone divorces their mate for any reason except sexual immorality and remarries, they commit adultery. What is even worse, according to Matthew 5:32, they may cause their mate to be guilty of adultery. Why? It should be considered that because God never intended for man or woman to live alone (Genesis 2:18), remarriage for one and possibly both parties is probably inevitable. For those already divorced, it should be emphasized that adultery is also forgivable. Although many consider divorced persons who remarry to be "living in sin" Scripture denies it:

> *Marriage is honorable in all, and the bed undefiled: But whoremongers and adulterers God will judge. (Hebrews 13:4 KJV.)*

All must accept the fact that when God's laws are broken, judgment and punishment will occur. Certainly adultery is punishable by God, and those who go from one sexual relationship to another committing adultery (whoremongers) will be judged accordingly.

Some hold to the concept that a legal termination of a marriage does not terminate the marriage under the laws of God until death intervenes even when immorality has occurred. But this is not true. The emphasis of these Scriptures is not upon the fact that God does not accept or acknowledge the legal termination of a marriage but rather the emphasis is on the fact that this is not what God intended in the beginning nor his ideal

Even though man is admonished that "... *What therefore God hath joined together, let not man put asunder (Matthew 19:6 (KJV),*" it is evident that man can terminate a marriage through a legal action and God accepts that termination as binding. This is evidenced by the fact that Joseph, who was a righteous man, planned to divorce Mary when she was found to be with child (Matthew 1:19) and naturally thought, by Joseph, to have committed adultery. Adultery was at that time punishable by death, and apparently he cared a great deal for her because he did not want to publicly embarrass or humiliate her, so he considered divorcing her privately. The betrothal period was considered as binding as marriage even though the marriage had not yet been consummated by the sexual act when, according to Matthew 19:5, a man and woman become one flesh.

Those contemplating divorce should consider that even though divorce for sexual immorality is permitted, Scripture does not require anyone to divorce their mate because of it. God's ideal is always forgiveness and continuation of a marriage relationship if possible rather than divorce.

But the legal termination of any marriage should be accepted as final as death if either party remarries. Scripture states if a man divorced his wife and he or she remarried and that subsequent marriage is terminated by death or divorce, the first husband should not take her back because that is an abomination in the sight of God (Deuteronomy 24:2-4). An abomination is defined as an extreme loathing. This indicates that to hold onto the false hope that the original marriage relationship can be restored or should be restored after either party has remarried is against Biblical teachings. Regardless of who sought the divorce, there are very few instances where either party is entirely blameless. It would be constructive to look within to discover what quality or fault caused their mate to seek a divorce so as to learn and benefit from that experience and not repeat that same mistake again.

With the ever rising divorce rate, the question is asked over and over: Why get married at all? The 1970s and 1980s heralded in a new era called the "New Morality" in which live-in situations became prevalent. Some contend that a piece of paper doesn't make a marriage or a difference in a relationship so long as there is commitment. This is just not true. You can have a perfectly legal and binding marriage without any sexual relationship as evidenced by those incapacitated by disease or injury. You can have a sexual relationship without a legal binding marriage, but you cannot have a marriage simply by having a sexual relationship. The so-called commitment in these situations is usually short lived.

There are many reasons why someone would not want the permanence of marriage. This type of commitment is usually, but not always, for the convenience of ending the relationship with as little inconvenience as possible with no long-term consequences such as a life-long commitment required by the marriage contract. However, because of emotional involvement, I am told that the pain of separation for the caring partner is the same as that suffered in divorce.

The bottom line is that many of these relationships are based on the theory that this person is good enough to live with to fill a temporary need but not good enough to marry. The basic truth is that if a man truly loves a woman, he will marry her. If he doesn't, she would do well to forget it rather than settle for second best. It is usually the woman who sells herself short in live-in situations. Of course, there are always exceptions. Also, all must acknowledge that God's laws say sexual relationships outside of marriage are wrong, and the laws of God never change. They were the same yesterday, are the same today, and will be the same tomorrow. We can ignore them much to our own detriment, we can break them, but we cannot change them.

The answer to why one should marry is very basic. Except for the few that God has chosen for celibacy for the primary purpose of serving him, God himself instilled in man an inherent need for a mate when he said, *"And the Lord God said, "It is not good for man to be alone; I will make a help meet for him (Genesis 2:18 (KJV)."* Thus it soon becomes apparent that from an early age the primary goal in life is to find that special someone to share our life.

Many are unable to find suitable mates and must resign themselves to a state of singleness and loneliness; therefore, those fortunate enough to have happy stable marriages should count their blessings and thank God every day.

The stigma of divorce of fifty years ago has largely been removed. It is unfortunate that even though the stigma has been removed, there are still a few who feel so complacently secure in their marriages that they look down on the divorced not realizing that there are many life situations which become intolerable even though there has been no sexual immorality. Those persons who sneer at the divorced forget that all mankind lives in continual sin, *". . . . For all have sinned and come short of the glory of God (Romans*

*3:23 (KJV)."* The assumption should never be made that if all mankind are sinners, they would be any greater sinner for having suffered through the tragedy of divorce. It could happen to anyone!

In a discussion about children with one of my co-workers during my engagement to be married in early 1950, they made the remark that they would never name a child after the father because if they got a divorce that would always be an unhappy reminder. Expressing all the wisdom of an eighteen-year-old, I replied, "That will not affect me. I shall never be divorced because I do not believe in divorce." Ten years later, it happened to me. Did I realize that my future mate was mentally ill in the 1950s? No, but I saw some signs and ignored them.

About fifteen years after the breakup of my marriage, divorce happened to one of my best friends. Myrtie, a friend of some twenty-five years, called and asked if I could meet her in nearby Fort Worth. Once there, she poured out her hurt and anguish over the fact that her husband of over twenty years and the father of five children was leaving her and no amount of pleading on her part could change his mind. And the tears flowed as she, too, was learning the bitter lesson that what cannot be cured must be endured. And she, too, was finding that it is the enduring that is the most difficult; that no matter how great a sorrow we carry inside, life goes on around us. Later, Myrtie did remarry and rebuild her life.

The only solution to any tragedy, divorce or otherwise, is to go forward by following the advice of Paul the apostle when he said, *". . . . Forgetting the past and looking forward to what lies ahead, I strain to reach the end of the race and receive the prize for which God is calling us up to heaven because of what Christ Jesus did for us." (Philippians 3:13-14 LB)*. The race, of course, is life here on earth with God at its center. Then God will sustain us through all of life's situations, even tragedy. Tragedies and heartache pale in comparison to the prize God has for God centered lives.

And finally, the **word divorce** means to disunite, sever, sunder. Many who suddenly find themselves confronted with divorce, especially those not wishing it, find it difficult to accept the finality of divorce and rebuild their lives on this basis. They mourn what they once had that is irrevocably lost to them. Rather than move forward to a new beginning, they would rather hold on to their hurt and wrap themselves in a cloak of bitterness and self-pity than to let go of what they cannot change. In these cases, it is difficult to think of anything else and put the past behind and rebuild. But it can be done! On those things which are irretrievable, it serves no worthwhile purpose to dwell on them becoming bitter and unhappy.

Children of all ages are also affected by divorce. Even some grown children feel their lives are ruined by their parents' actions because they no longer have their parents together as they once had or the childhood home to remember. What is even worse, some grown children blame parents for their own actions, faults, and failures. But they, too, should understand that when they reach young adulthood, it is not what parents or others have done but what they do that makes their individual life what it is. Becoming young adults, we become accountable to God for our own actions and what we make of the life he gave us.

In one of those many years past returning home from a rare trip to the Greenwood Community about six miles west of my home, I caught sight of a beautiful golden tree that towered at least twenty feet above the other trees. In Central Texas, there is mostly scrub oak that grows to about forty feet due to a lack of moisture and extended droughts. In the fall, the leaves turn from green to a stale brown and fall off most of the time. But this was one of those falls where the trees were a riot of color, and this great tree with the sun shinning on its brilliant yellow leaves sparkled like a crown. Because it was so beautiful, I wondered whose tree it was and decided to drive past my house if necessary to find who it belonged to; and I kept watching for it.

Every time I went down a hill, I lost sight of it; but every time I topped the next hill, I sighted it again. When finally I reached this beautiful tree, I was astounded to find that it was the great cottonwood that had stood in my sister's yard for the thirty or more years she had been living there which was only a block from my own home. Because of its location in the yard, it was not visible from the East which was the way I usually came home, so I had not noticed how it towered above the other trees nor its spectacular beauty. A few days later I saw my sister and told her that if she had not seen her tree from a distance coming from the West, she should drive to the Greenwood Community just so she could see how beautiful it was before the leaves fell off. Sister smiled and said, "I saw it the other day as I was coming home. And I, too, had decided to drive until I found whose tree it was; but when I got to it, I discovered that it had been mine all along.

God is like that great towering tree with its golden crown. If we can just lift our eyes above the hills of our struggles, our heartache, and our tragedies, we will see that God is there towering above all else. Even though we may not be able to see from the distance that he stands in our yard, when we finally top that last hill we will know he was there all that time. And when we finally stand at his feet, we will have reached, as I had at that time, the place where there is no pain from old hurts and old wounds have healed.

I wasted so many years crying because I had not learned how to put the past behind and go forward. I cried in my own pain, but tears do not change harsh realities. I cried over shattered illusions, broken dreams, and lost love, but that did not change them. I cried over a situation I could not help nor change once it had happened. I cried because I had no one to share my life. But most of all, I cried because my own poor choices were the cause of the situation in which I found myself that left my son without a father.

But now, many years later, I can truthfully say: Don't cry for me! Cry for the one whose life was overshadowed by mental illness until his death. Cry for the mother who wept for her mentally ill son, as I wept for mine during his growing-up years because he had no father. When I reflect back, it is as if past tragedies never happened. Through an expanse of many years, God truly healed my life. And my early adult life that began as a journey through the valley of heartache and tears became an adventure of searching to find what God had for me.

# Chapter 4

## THE SEARCH FOR TOMORROW

Relocating in early 1979 from Central Texas to Eastern Arkansas, I was starting a whole new adventure in the excitement of beginning my first job as an official court reporter to work in criminal and civil court. Generally getting resettled in my new world, I joined a local church and inquired as to whether they had a Sunday school class for single adults in which I could participate, and, it being a small town, was told that they did not.

    I loved the class and teacher in which I was enrolled, but I wanted to join in some of the activities provided by the larger churches for single adults. So I visited the famous Bellview Baptist Church in nearby Memphis, Tennessee in which they had a department called New Life consisting of approximately three or four hundred single adults. Their organization was one of the most impressive I had ever attended. Once I attended one of their class socials which consisted of a potluck supper, singing, and later a sharing time. I sat spellbound as some shared their hurts, sorrows, and how much just knowing someone was there who cared and how having others to share their problems with had helped them.

    Later, reflecting over this, I had a letdown feeling and began to wonder if this really was the right place for me. They had shared their problems but I didn't have any problems of that kind anymore. They had shared their hurts over broken relationships and loneliness, but I didn't have any hurts of that kind anymore either. Therefore, I felt I didn't have anything to share or contribute. Because this thought was depressing, it was pushed into the recesses of my mind and forgotten. Still later that year driving across Arkansas' beautiful Interstate 40 on my way to Eastern Oklahoma to visit my sister Mozelle, I was just driving along soaking up the beauty of the day, the sunshine and enjoying the peace of a nice quiet drive when suddenly it occurred to me: You have one thing to give—hope! Many single adults were at the place where I had been many, many years ago. I knew their pain. I knew their hurt. I had been there. What was the hope I had to give: The certainty of knowing that (1) time heals, (2) we can learn and profit from every experience, no matter how painful it is, and (3) this, too (hurt) shall pass away.

After visiting several times, it became obvious that Bellview was not the place for me. The distance was too great to travel frequently. A short time later my local church established a singles department, so I began working with single adults again. Life was exciting. I was busy. I loved my job. I now had time to do things I had wanted to do for a long time such as enrolling in a painting class. But regardless of what we have, the desire for someone to share our life continues. It was then that I learned about the miracles. The Oral Roberts ministry sent some literature with some sort of jingle or rhyme about seven miracles for 1980. The instructions were simple. Write down seven needs in which there is no humanly way possible to achieve them. Put them in a small envelope, seal it, place it in the Bible, and pray about the needs. Then at the end of the year, open it and see what God has accomplished.

Who believes in that kind of miracles? But why not try it? I wrote down needs concerning my family and friends, but what should I ask for myself? The only thing truly lacking was a husband. I had been asking God to send me someone suitable for nearly twenty-five years, and he hadn't, so why should he now? If he did, that would truly be a miracle! As the year of 1980 passed, almost everyone on my list received some special blessing, except me! But in February of 1980, James Chandler, a handsome, middle-aged man with a lot of what seemed to be good-husband qualities moved into the apartment complex three doors down from mine. All the single girls looked him over. But one Saturday as I looked out the window, I thought—he can't be too smart. He's moving a coffee table in, in the rain, getting it wet! A few weeks later we met in the parking lot early one morning on the way to work. He said, "Good morning." I said, "Hi."

Then one beautiful morning in May when I wasn't in court, Mrs. Palmer who was my next door neighbor and I were standing on the balcony leaning against my door just enjoying the sunshine and visiting when up drove James Chandler. Mrs. Palmer and I just stood there gaping as he walked across the parking lot. Dressed impeccably in the most gorgeous blue suit, his countenance somewhat sad, he seemed to be surrounded by the brightness of the sun. And the inaudible Voice that we always attribute to God said, "There is your future husband." I said to myself, "Are you sure, Lord? I don't know him, and he doesn't even know I'm alive."

As he came up the stairs, spoke, and disappeared into his apartment, Mrs. Palmer said, "He sure is good looking!" I said, "Oh, he is!" He later told me that he had been to a funeral and that was the reason he had returned home that morning. He also said that for months he had watched me go up and down the stairs through his window. Coming and going through the rest of that year, we spoke and visited on the stairs occasionally. Months later during the winter, I found the ice and snow scraped from my windshield each morning. In the parking lot one day, he asked if I liked barbecue; and I did. From time to time after that, he appeared at my door and said, "I brought you some barbecue." Each Time, I took his barbecue, thanked him, and closed the door.

One Saturday about noon when I was really busy, he appeared at my door. I took his barbecue, thanked him, and shut the door. About an hour after the job was finished, the surprised expression on his face penetrated my denseness. It suddenly occurred to me that he had wanted to share a sandwich "with" me. I went down to his apartment, knocked on his door and asked if I could fix him a sandwich out of his barbecue. He good-naturedly replied, "No, I just ate a bologna sandwich." On my way back to my apartment, the humor of the situation struck me as I thought of him all these months eating bologna sandwiches while I ate his barbecue. It hadn't occurred to me that he wanted to share it. I thought he was just being neighborly because he had not asked for a date. After that, occasionally he took me for a drive on beautiful Sunday afternoons or for ice cream. On Thanksgiving of 1981, he asked if he could take me out for Thanksgiving dinner, and we had our first real date.

Apartment living was not for me though on a long-term basis. I bought a small house and began remodeling it. Working on the house in my free time didn't leave too much time at the apartment. He started stopping by the new house, sometimes offering to help. Late one Saturday while cleaning the attic which was filled with soot from a previous fire, there was a loud knock on the door. Thinking it was the contractor, I climbed down from the attic and opened the door. Seeing that it was James, I just shut the door. As I opened the door again, we both broke into gales of laughter as he said, "Is that you behind all that soot?" The only thing visible behind my mask, scarf, soot, and dirt were my eyes. My friend Sharon Long who also lived in the apartment complex laughingly said, "It's got to be love; no guy would hang around anyone that looks like you do when you come home from working on that house if he weren't in love."

Finally the house was finished and I moved. We continued dating. We discussed marriage. We broke up several times—always with the phone calls, notes, and cute cards in between. When he went out of town on business, he brought me small gifts. When I went to Texas to visit my family, he called every night. Once when I went to Texas during one of those "off times," I returned to find a string of pearls in my mailbox. Who can stay mad at a guy who leaves a string of pearls (my favorite jewelry) in the mailbox?

My concerned neighbor Jean would never inquire directly, but occasionally in a worried tone she would say, "I haven't seen James around lately." To which I always replied, "Oh, we're not seeing each other right now." I laughingly told one of my friends who lived at Arkadelphia that I should put a sign on the front porch that said off/on so the neighbors would know our current status without having to ask.

My family also followed with great interest the progress of our relationship since this was the first man I had shown more than a passing interest in for many years. My niece Doris who is also a best friend has the uncanny ability of finding humorous cards that portray a particular situation. She sent James a birthday card depicting a basin of water with the stopper pulled out and a fast-moving whirlpool in which a man in a fishing boat was rowing for his life. The caption stated, "Keep paddlin'!" Months later, he laughingly said, "That's just the way I feel sometimes," as he showed it to me. After we were married, along with her gift, Doris sent another card which showed a bride and groom in a fishing boat on very smooth water in a lake. She wrote, "See how calm the waters are."

In the meantime, the off/on situation continued and our relationship didn't seem to be going anywhere. But my mischievous nature surfaced occasionally. Once when he hadn't called for several days, I sent him a card showing one blade of grass with a ladybug on it that said, "How's every little thing?" One Christmas during one of those "off periods," I sent him a beautifully wrapped box to his place of business where he managed a farm equipment center with the message written on the outside, "The perfect gift for the guy who has everything—except one." (Meaning me)! I imagined the humor it would create with all his employees when he opened it. Inside was a jewelry box with a nose ring in it. He outsmarted me though; he didn't open it there.

As time progressed, both of us knew this off/on situation could not continue. A relationship can only be maintained for a reasonable time without marriage. There had been no doubt in my mind that we were right for each other, but I began to question whether I had heard right when God said, "This is your new husband." Perhaps I had misunderstood. One Saturday, as the situation was discussed, the decision was made to stop seeing each other permanently. I was heartbroken but could see no other solution. I managed to teach my Sunday school class the next morning; but as my best friend Jane and I walked down the stairs and stood in the hall talking, the tears that could no longer be contained streamed down my face as I told her of that decision. For three long, silent, miserable weeks, we did not see each other. No phone calls, no cute cards, and no notes.

Because I missed him picking me up after church for our regular Sunday luncheon date, that third Sunday of this silence I stayed at church talking to every friend I had to postpone going home as long as possible. It was a quarter to one when I finally turned the corner and saw his car parked in front of my house waiting for me. The clouds of gloom suddenly lifted, the sun shinned brighter, and it was a beautiful day. He said, "I missed you." I said, "I missed you, too, but I wasn't going to tell you." To which he replied, "That's what I thought." The next week, I went to Texas for a few days to visit my family. When I came back on Sunday, he took me out to eat and simply said, "Will you marry me?" And I said, "Yes." Three weeks later, after a whirlwind of preparation, we were married.

Did we live happily every after? Happy, yes, but there were the usual adjustments to be made when two individual personalities are merged. We agreed that if we disagreed we would not fight as fighting is counterproductive. My friends were much amused as I told them, "He likes to fish, and so if he gets mad he said he is going fishing. I love yard work, so if I get mad I am going to work in the yard. Being an avid fisherman, no one will probably know he is mad because he goes fishing all the time; but if you see me out mowing the yard with snow on the ground, you will know that I am mad."

I remember the now amusing tree incident that needed a limb cut off. James said to call someone. But who can you get to come and lop of one small limb, so utilizing the agility and residual expertise of my childhood tomboy days, I shinnied up the tree and sawed the limb off while he was at work. Later, after being lectured on the improprieties of a fifty-four-year-old woman climbing trees, I concluded that my new husband was very upset with me. But I didn't really know how upset he was until my friends Lou Ann and Kenneth Locke who lived in Arkadelphia stopped by on their way to Memphis. They had stopped by James' place of business on the way and laughingly told me that he had said, "Charlene is not in court today, so she will be at home. You might find her hanging from a limb, but she'll be there."

As was my usual custom when things were not exactly to my liking, I complained to the Lord saying, "Lord, why did you give me this contrary man that does not want me to, of all things, climb trees?" Then I smiled recalling a previous conversation with my boss, the judge, when he had asked why I had not remarried. I started listing all the qualities of character I wanted in a husband. He had said, "Good grief! You're not looking for a man; you're looking for a saint."

Over the years, my family's thinking was that there was no one that could cope with my perfectionism's. But that wasn't the real reason I had found no one. The main reason was that in every man I dated, if he exhibited one little character flaw of what I "thought" pointed toward mental instability, I crossed him off. I had had enough of coping with mental instabilities to last me a lifetime. For the husband I had asked for, God had given me the best he had available in qualities of character. So I decided not to climb trees again, at lease until he became used to the idea. That was several years ago. He has adjusted admirably to my perfectionism's, and I have adjusted tolerably well to the "don't do's."

Do I still pray and practice these principles that first put me in touch with God, including the miracles? The answer is an emphatic yes. Do they still work? The answer again is an emphatic yes. Are all my prayers answered in the way I ask? No, of course not. Do all the miracles listed come to pass? No, but each year in whatever Sunday school class I am teaching, we do the miracles and wait for God to act. Through the years, the results told me by others are uncanny. A **word of caution** pertaining to the miracles: Do not expect God to fill the need or solve the problem as you plan or think because when God acts, it is in a better and completely unexpected manner.

It became obvious that the small house I had bought before our marriage was too small. It was bursting at the seams. I proceeded to ask God for a rambling old house in the country with a winding lane leading up to it. For two years, nothing happened. Then the real estate agent showed me a house. There it was, the curved lane, the country, the beautiful trees—not the house that I had asked for but one that would better suit our needs. It was disappointing that the price was beyond our limits. I kept emphasizing that if this was the right house, God would make a way. Meanwhile, we continued looking but found nothing we liked. Another year passed, and the price dropped to what we had originally offered. After paint, wallpaper, and a lot of work, this house proved to suit our needs perfectly, the right size, a good location in the country, and finally affordable.

Surrounded by the flowers, trees, a job that I loved and someone to share my life along with all the other blessings we received, I suddenly realized that the search for tomorrow had become the reality of today!

## Chapter 5

### BALANCE THE SCALE

If there is anything we need in this hectic chaotic world in which we live today, it is a sense of balance. There is balance in all the laws of nature. God created perfect balance and harmony in his universe. It is the imbalance we humans create that cause most of our problems; therefore, the more balance we have in all areas of our life, the fewer our problems.

In the early 1970s, I once remarked to my sister Fay that I could have done better if circumstances had been more ideal. Then as the realization suddenly occurred to me, I said, "But circumstances are never ideal." If we are to achieve a sense of balance, it is in spite of circumstances, not because of them.

It has been said that I raised my son Mark alone since he was five. It is true that I had no financial help, but I cannot truthfully say that I raised him alone. This was at a time when the facade I presented to the world covered a personality so shy and timid that I hardly spoke to anyone. It was only in looking back over an expanse of many, many years that I could see how God had balanced our lives. When one thing was missing, God provided another.

Because of his mental illness, the husband and father was missing from our home; therefore, there was imbalance. But while I had to work, God filled the gaps when I could not be there to care for Mark. It was my sister Fay, who is now ninety years old, who kept him when he was sick, included us in family gatherings, holidays, and outings at the lake, and so many other things. We both treasure these memories.

There was the late Dow Jordan who had the Kindergarten and Day Care Center and became one of my dearest friends. There was her husband Bob. Because I had to leave for work so early, Bob took Mark to school every morning. This was special to Mark.

There was Dr. Merrick who doctored our colds and flu and helped keep us healthy.

There was Mrs. Wilson and Mr. Clay who taught children in Sunday school. Shortly before Mark was baptized when he was six and the pastor was counseling him, the pastor asked who his Sunday school teacher was. He replied, "Beth Wilson's mother, but they took her away from me." He had been promoted to another class and did not understand why Mrs. Wilson was not his teacher any more. To him, it was a personal loss.

Then there was Martha McClung who also taught Sunday school and worked with the children in church. She took them on field trips each week all during the summers when school was out so they wouldn't get bored. This was the highlight of Mark's week during those summers.

And there was Dr. McIntosh and his office staff who repaired our teeth. Once when Mark got soaking wet walking from school to keep a dental appointment, he came home and said, "Mother, Mrs. McIntosh took "me" back to school because it was raining. That was very special to him. Once it was Emma Lou, one of the staff, that hurriedly rushed him up to the church after his summer dental appointment for one of Mrs. McClung's field trips because he didn't have time to walk the three blocks after they finished with his teeth. They weren't expected to do these things; they just did them.

Later, there was Tommy Coker the music director who worked and inspired them during the teen years to develop their talents and informed me that Mark really could sing.

There were so many more who worked in the church over the years teaching and providing many varied activities for the children.

There was also Ada Lois Williamson, my faithful Sunday school teacher, who shared seats and blankets and provided rides to out-of-town football games when Mark and her daughter June played in the high school band so I could attend them.

In the long and adventurous journey through life, countless others, in addition to family, teachers, co-workers, and friends, touched us in a meaningful way also providing a treasury of memories. What would I have done without this balance God provided through all these great and special people? It is a sobering thought that we, in turn, touch the lives of others; but do we touch their life for good as all these great people touched ours?

When faced with the storms of life, there is a tendency to ask how we got to the place where we are, just as I did time after time. Even though it is obvious it is probably because of some choice we made, there is yet another lesson to be learned: You can only be creative and filed with joy and happiness when you **bloom where you're planted** regardless of circumstances. My life, at that extremely difficult time, can be compared with soil that is so rocky, barren, and desolate it seems nothing could possibly grow. Yet, occasionally in these places, there is one small beautiful flower growing among the rocks in practically no soil. Why would one tiny flower bother to bloom in the midst of all that desolation? It is amazing the difference that one tiny bloom makes in the starkness of the landscape. So it is with the life that blooms where it is planted . . . . Through the many years of spiritual growth and God's help, this is what I hope I have done!

One summer, I phoned my now grown son who was co-owner of Denali Wilderness Safaris and struggling to start a new business, a river boat excursion tour up the Denali River that circles the famous Mt. McKinley National Park in Alaska. When asked how he was doing, he replied, "Fine, but right now I'm living a hand-to-mouth existence." I said, "Yes, your mouth, God's hand. We've always lived that way." Needless to say, whatever the future holds for either of us, the one thing that I hope never changes is this hand-to-mouth existence, our mouth, God's hand!

# *Postscript 2006*

God works in mysterious ways! Today, looking back through the years, I not only see God continuously working in my life but in the life of my son. Mark had worked for Frank Rosenbaugh for years in Anchorage before Mr. Rosenbaugh moved to Seattle. Mr. Rosenbaugh asked Mark to move to Seattle and continue working for him, but Mark was unable to move because he was still involved with his summer business.

Then in the summer of 1991, a beautiful young lady named Nancy Jones went to Alaska for a fun summer working for Princess Tours with which Mark's business coordinated. They met and had a fun summer dating. Where was Nancy from? Seattle. In 1993 Mark sold his business and house and moved to Seattle. He again worked for Mr. Rosenbaugh managing Northern Lights Service Center for several years. Mark and Nancy were married in 1995. Their first child Dana Lauren was born August 13, 1998. Their second baby Susan Emmy was born March 18, 2003.

Mark is presently employed by the Ford Motor Company Dealership near his home, and Nancy is employed by the National Oceanic Atmospheric Administration. They still reside in Seattle.

# About the Author

Charlene Hoglan Roberson Chandler is a native Texan and teacher of Bible study classes in churches for over 35 years. Employed by the Department of Army at Fort Wolters, Texas from 1962 to 1974. Upon base closure, attended and graduated from Chapman Court Reporting College in Fort Worth, Texas. Relocated to Forrest City, Arkansas in 1979 for employment in the First Judicial Circuit of Eastern Arkansas as an official court reporter for the Honorable Henry Wilkinson, retiring in 1995. She married James Chandler in 1984. Children consist of three wonderful stepchildren and one special son Mark who resides in Seattle with his wife and two daughters. Hobbies consist of oil painting, writing, reading, sewing, and flower gardening. Mrs. Chandler is author of Tribulation, Closer Than We Think and a full-color illustrated book for children The Beginning of Christmas, A Story for the Young and Old. Email: *crobchandler@sbcglobal.net*

# *Endnotes*

1. Love or Perish by Dr. Smiley Blanton. Fawcett World Library Publishers, 67 W. 44th St. New York, N.Y. Paperback. Introductions and Page 17.
2. The Power of Positive Thinking by Norman Vincent Peale. 1956. Prentice-Hall, Inc., Englewood Cliffs, N.J.
3. Love Comes First In Creative Living by Norman Vincent Peale. Peale Center, Box 8000, Paling, N.Y. 12564. Plus. 11F70/Vol.23/No. 4(Part 1).
4. Wanda McIntosh, West Helena, Arkansas. Her name used by permission.
5. Get Rid of Resentment by Dr. James A. Stringham, Houston, Texas. Guideposts, 39 Seminary Hill Road, Carmel, N.Y. 10512. May, 1973. Page 20.
6. Beyond Ourselves by Catherine Marshall. Baker Book House, P.O. Box 6287, Grand Rapids, Michigan 49516. Paperback. Chapter 4. Page 68.
7. Thought Conditioners. Peale Center, P.O. Box 8000, Pawling, N,Y. 12564.
8. The Power of Positive Praying by John Bisagno. 1965. Zondervan Publishing House, 5300 Patterson Avenue S.E., Grand Rapids, Michigan 49530.
9. All Things are possible Through Prayer by Charles Allen. Fleming H. Revell, a division of Baker Book House, P.O. Box 6287, Grand Rapids, Michigan 49516-6287.
10. This Thing Called Guidance by Ruth Stafford Peale. Peale Center, P.O. Box 8000, Pawling, N.Y. 12564. Plus. Vol. 22/No.8 (Part 11).
11. Insight That Sees Through Confusion by Norman Vincent Peale. Peale Center, P.O. Box 8000, Pawling, N.Y. 12564. Plus. 40c70/Vol. 22/No. 8 (Part 111)
12. How Do You Know You're in Love. The American Institute of Family Relations, 5287 Sunset Boulevard, Los Angeles, CA 90027, Publication No. 26, By Paul Popenoe, Sc.D.

BVG